AF596805

DIVINITY SCHOOL

Book of Poems

ABOUT THE AUTHOR

Elizabeth Pyjov is a poet, graduate school professor, renowned teacher of meditation, scholar, speaker, theologian, and lawyer who holds three Harvard degrees, speaks five languages, has lived in seven countries, and has designed over 250 programs to guide individuals in finding happiness and fulfillment through her organization Happiness Sangha. Her passion is to make the world more compassionate by helping people practice self-compassion.

In these poems, Elizabeth combines what she learned about ritual and meaning at Harvard Divinity School, what she learned about neuroscience at Stanford Medical School, her literature degree from Harvard College, the rigor of Harvard Law School, and her time studying with Buddhist teachers such as the Dalai Lama, Thich Nhat Hanh, and Jon Kabat-Zinn.

Elizabeth is currently a law school professor at Chicago Loyola where she teaches compassion and leadership, and a business school professor at the Loyola School of Business where she lectures on leadership of self. She has taught at places like Harvard University, Stanford University, Columbia University, the New York Supreme Court, and the Library of Congress. Reinterpreting ancient wisdom to make it accessible to us today is the greatest privilege of her life. *Divinity School* is her first volume of poetry.

DIVINITY SCHOOL

Book of Poems

Buddhist Reinterpretation of Judeo-Christian Theology

ELIZABETH PYJOV

Foreword by Michael Puett
Afterword by Luis Fernández Cifuentes

ISBN 979-8-218-89133-6 (hardcover)
ISBN 979-8-218-89134-3 (ebook)

Cover design by Elizabeth Pyjov

Published by Happiness Sangha Printing Press
www.happinessangha.com
elizabeth.pyjov@gmail.com
Printed in the USA

Contents

Dedicated with immense gratitude
to my teachers and professors.
Thank you for your love, wisdom,
and kindness.

Out beyond ideas
of wrongdoing
and rightdoing,
there is a field.

I'll meet you there.

—*Rumi*

FOREWORD

Elizabeth Pyjov is a practitioner of meditation and compassion. She is a professor, scholar, renowned teacher, theologian, independent thinker, and an extraordinary poet.

Through her work, she has explored spiritual practices across geographies and ages. Conversations with Elizabeth will commonly range over Ancient Greek and Indian mythology, modern psychology, Buddhist thought, legal theory, science of the mind, rabbinic Judaism, and early Christian visions of divinization.

In this collection of 44 poems, Elizabeth explores theology and cosmology across several of these traditions through an unconventional lens. When Elizabeth was a student in my Classical Chinese Philosophy class (at the time she was a graduate student at both Harvard Law School and a Master's student in theology at Harvard Divinity School), she would share with me her modern and poetic rethinking of these ancient traditions. I greatly enjoyed listening to them. In this book she now shares them with you.

The academic rigor she brings to the discussion serves as a backbone and structure to rediscovering truths that are timeless. Rather than a theological analysis, she offers poetic reflections infused with Buddhist concepts, chronicling her own journey from a Judeo-Christian mindset to a largely Hindu-Buddhist way of thought.

This crossroads speaks to the heart of her biography. Elizabeth was born in Moscow, Russia. She grew up in the Eastern Orthodox tradition in Silicon Valley, California. At age 16, she started a daily mindfulness practice, and in her early 20s, she became very serious about her compassion and self-compassion practice, thanks to her work with the Stanford Center for Compassion and Altruism Research and Education. After discovering that about half of her roots are Jewish, she began reading Jewish texts and studying Jewish traditions. Then while at Harvard Divinity School (where these poems were written, hence the title) she focused on Buddhism, Hinduism, and Ancient Chinese philosophy. Along the way, she studied neuroscience at Stanford Medical School, conducted legal investigations for the state of New York, worked in human rights at the United Nations in Geneva, served as a translator to Nobel Prize-winning Italian playwright Dario Fo, and even practiced investment fund law at a top law firm.

What makes her vision stand out is that she knows the world from many angles. Her way of thinking is multi-disciplinary by nature. She wrestles with ancient traditions seriously. She dives deeply into them, and reinterprets them with a sense of humor that turns preconceptions, beliefs, and traditions on their head. She is rethinking subversively and yet respectfully institutionalized forms of Judaism and Christianity.

In the first few poems, she explores biblical figures through a Buddhist lens. The framing of the poetry cycle takes us from God (poem one) to the Buddha (poem 44). In the first poem, we begin with a journey of self-realization even for God:

> Somewhere in the
> darkness
> there was a being
> meditating on light
>
> Let there be light he
> said
> and he turned into
> God.

Here God's act of creation of light is a simultaneous act of self-discovery. Through transformation of self, he turned into God. This is in line with the Buddhist idea that one isn't bestowed divinity but cultivates and discovers it in oneself through one's thoughts, words, and actions—in other words, through what one practices.

This Buddhist reinterpretation of Judeo-Christian theology continues in the second poem with an unconventional view on the classic story of the fall:

Maybe Eve left paradise on her own
to get away from Adam.
But he loved her and followed.

Or maybe she thought
"Living in paradise—how bourgeois.
Goodbye to this sleepy life."

But most likely she matured
more quickly—women do—
and saw that paradise is fiction.

Eve chooses to leave paradise because she's seeking something more than eternal bliss. The poem paints her as an active, rebellious figure who leaves paradise because it hinders her growth–it is a construct that does not allow space for her evolution. She chooses to embrace reality and the full spectrum of human experience, including joy and sorrow, complexity and risk. And perhaps here she didn't even like Adam that much to begin with!

Many poems invite us to step outside judgment and connect to common humanity. In the poem "St. Thomas," Elizabeth puts an emphasis on learning from direct experience as Thomas questions sacred teachings. (And, of course, so does Elizabeth). Here doubt isn't seen as a weakness, but instead as a necessary step to genuine understanding. Thomas trusts his senses more than teachings or dogma—an ultimate expression of freedom. Indeed, only in a non-dogmatic framework can an individual connect to oneself.

In the poem "Judas," Elizabeth takes a compassionate approach toward the most controversial figure in Christian theology, suggesting that we are all capable of betrayal. We have all betrayed ourselves and others many times.

Some poems hit us in the gut.

From the perspective of a female spiritual practitioner, how might we understand Mary Magdalene?

> Magdalene is a saint
> because what greater suffering
> than to love a holy man?

Through recontextualizing religion and religious figures in this way, we get to breathe new power, new life, and new dimensions into what can seem outdated or obscure. The strange, extraordinary and at times frightening power of these traditions allows us to encounter the world around us anew.

Through Elizabeth's words, what has been discussed at length throughout history is not stale anymore. Ancient philosophies and practices come to life again. Along with a scholarly preparation, she brings you along on a search for meaning and engagement with an open heart.

Compassion and a humanistic worldview run through the poems. Along the way, she captures in brief poems the heart of Buddhist thought—not as a religion, but a way of looking at the world—without compromising the complexity of Buddhist cosmology.

In our times, multiplicity is increasingly relevant. This collection is an invitation to stop grasping the world as stable categories: "endless gods / and the possibilities become endless." Today we sometimes discount a polytheistic worldview as primitive. Elizabeth points out instead "many gods, many truths"—again, a pathway for the individual to be true to oneself. In connecting to oneself, we connect to the divine.

Poems were originally a way to connect to the divine, and *Divinity School* brings us back to those roots of poetry. Of course the fullness of spiritual knowledge lies outside words, and yet words can call us to it. As a practitioner of meditation, Elizabeth knows well how one re-encounters the world by transcending words and following the rhythms of one's breathing. These poems are based upon that same rhythm of the breath, allowing the reader to witness the world through meditation. The reader will encounter a sharp clarity and a rhythmic flow that brings a reverence to both what is intellectual and what is flesh and blood—and an unwavering optimism in relation to the messiness of life.

Elizabeth brings inspiration from her knowledge of Russian poetry (as a native Russian speaker), and her study of Ancient Greek, Latin, Sanskrit, Pali, Italian, Spanish, and French poetry. When she was an undergraduate at Harvard, she was the only student to take advanced literature classes in seven different languages. (As a freshman, she got perfect scores in the Latin and Ancient Greek placement exams.) In reading these poems, one sees the workings of a brilliant scholar, a brilliant theologian, and a brilliant poet.

Elizabeth evokes a serenity that allows us to embrace opposites and be on intimate terms with both the darkness and the vibrancy of the cosmos. Of course, the macrocosm outside us mirrors the microcosm within us. Her work today is letting every part of the individual be a pathway to self-compassion, taking us from a limited mind to a heart as wide as the world. Reading carefully, we might touch the infinity outside ourselves and the infinities within. As John Ashbery wrote: "until only infinity remained of beauty."

These poems communicate a life philosophy from a seasoned thinker. Elizabeth is the rare intellectual with sensuality and a love of life, with an unwavering commitment to finding both meaning and joy—and helping others find it as well. As I know from Elizabeth's work and as you the reader will now know from her poems, she embodies a luminous, non-dogmatic sense of endless possibilities and a deep attention to what makes us both human and divine. These poems too will give you access to your own freedom.

In one of our office hour discussions, Elizabeth once said to me that the most liberating teaching for her is that "We are not here to judge, we are here to pay attention."

That is indeed a path to freedom. In one of her poems, Elizabeth states:

> The art is not writing
> it's witnessing.
>
> The art is not painting
> it's seeing.
>
> The art is not singing
> it's hearing.
>
> The art is not doing
> it's being.

The entire collection is just this. As she describes in her poem "Art," she is not writing, she is witnessing. She is not painting, she is seeing. She is not singing, she is hearing. She is not doing, she is being. She opens the door to our heightened awareness as well. We can joyfully accept the invitation.

Michael Puett
Cambridge MA, 2025

Harvard University, Chair of the Committee on the Study of Religion, Walter C. Klein Professor of Chinese History and Anthropology, and the Director of the Asia Center

DIVINITY SCHOOL

Book of Poems

GOD

Somewhere in the
darkness
there was a being
meditating on light

Let there be light he
said
and he turned into
God.

EVE

Maybe Eve left paradise on her own
to get away from Adam.
But he loved her and followed.

Or maybe she thought
"Living in paradise—how bourgeois.
Goodbye to this sleepy life."

But most likely she matured
more quickly—women do—
and saw that paradise is fiction.

GABRIEL

"Mary I don't know how to say this but…"

The young woman looked up.

"Having faith
is easy,
it's just
letting go
of our resistance
to receiving."

She saw a sky
not of clouds
but of
angels

like vultures
circling
prey.

JOSEPH

Mary with the infant
A donkey and an ox
Some Magi and a camel
Shepherds, sheep and angels

Looking out at the nativity scene
"Not my circus, not my monkeys."

ST. PETER

The man who denied Christ started the church.
He denied Christ three times
and then, starting the church,
a fourth.

CHRIST

The Bible does not describe
what Christ looks like,
    his face
    his frown
    his smile.
We just know he was
    magnetic
    enigmatic
    free.

Let's stop calling
Christ a saviour
because
    saviours
    create
    victims.

And victims are never free,
just like saviours.

ST. THOMAS

"Lord, we don't know where you're going,
how can we know the way?"

Thomas did not believe until he saw,
until he touched.
He wanted experience,
to feel against his rough fingers
the imprint of the nail
in Christ's flesh.
One carpenter touching
the body of another.

"You're my Lord because I think so,
not because everyone else does."

Doubt, the twin of belief.

Yet he was the first to
acknowledge Christ's
divinity. He was the only one
ready to die with Christ,
the only one
Mary appeared to
after she died.

JUDAS

Should we judge Judas?
What one judges one becomes.
We are all betrayer and betrayed,
a natural consequence
of an immortal soul.
You have sold yours
many times.

Shinran the Japanese monk
ate meat and the nun Enshini
was his wife.
There is no room for the practitioner
to be concerned about
being good and bad, he said.

Is there room for the apostle?

Out beyond ideas of wrongdoing
and rightdoing, there is a field.
Meet Rumi there.
Meet Shinran there.
Meet Judas there.

MARY MAGDALENE

Magdalene is a saint
because what greater suffering
than to love a holy man?

PONTIUS PILATE

Didn't know
a merciful attitude
usually achieves
more accurate
results

that rules have
no existence
outside of
individuals

that when we're
judging we're not
paying attention.

MARY

I gave him life
He gave me the sense of
          eternal life
A fair exchange, wouldn't you say?

Anyway I loved him
but didn't love my son being a zealot
(the water to wine piece was nice).

He was crucified—
this means
the world is
losing its
innocence at
immeasurable
speed.

He was crucified—
it hurts to say it.

HOLY SPIRIT

Everywhere, and

no more hidden

than the air itself.

Also, breath.

BIBLE

The text is inexhaustible. You can swim in
it and never get to the bottom of it.
They say the writers did this on purpose,
layer upon layer.

Is it because there is so much biblical meaning?
Or is it because we are so good at reading meaning into text,

well-experienced with reading
into our own existence.

BIBLICAL TEXT

The text wraps the space
between heaven and earth—
touching heaven, it helps
us see it and yet
hides it, shelters it, covers
it up.
Beautiful and translucent
barrier.

LANGUAGE

Language carries within it
unconscious limitations,
all misuses, linguistically
all misuses, socially.
Language like money
has heavy karma.

WORDS

synthesis and simplification
          how sweet
synthesis and simplification
          how useless

what do we do with speech
tools of
synthesis and
simplification
of false
uncomplication

ART

The art is not writing
it's witnessing

The art is not painting
it's seeing

The art is not singing
it's hearing

The art is not doing
it's being

RELIGION

Religion is filled with
pain, pleasure and beauty—
all attention-grabbing devices.

Each religion,
a local religion
every moment
every morning.

Every morning
our attention
new.

HUMAN TRAGEDY

Birds fly by
in a world of endless flux

Seasons change
in a world of endless flux

The earth cools and heats up
in a world of endless flux

Our desire to find permanence for ourselves
in this endless world of flux.

HOW MANY GODS

No end

No beginning

Evolution, devolution

Contraction, expansion

Expansion, contraction

Is it infinite or is it

calculable?

Does the world fit

in one mind or does

it not? Does it

fit in the mind of God,

is someone keeping track?

How many gods do we

need for someone to keep

track of the universe?

MOTHERLY LOVE

We and motherly love
are made for each other and
where that bond fails
human life fails.

If you can't love your mother
you can love
          Hera
          the Madonna
          the Earth itself.

When we love our mother, we feel peace.

When we don't, we feel
          abstract vagueness
          blank productivity
          compulsive sympathy
          malign curiosity.

The light still glows
          in a whiff, melancholy way.

We say some pretty critical things just to defend ourselves
not guilty, not frightened, not shaken, not disgusted

we dance around frantically like a wild animal,

we hope we'll soon be ourselves again
          in a weary banality that reminds us of death.

ANCIENT GREECE

If obeying one god
    displeases another
if piety toward one is
    offense to another
the world becomes flexible
the colors come alive with
    nuance
        moral possibility
            ethical imagination.

One god, one truth
many gods, many truths.

One god, one possibility
    endless gods
        and the possibilities
            become endless.

100 YEARS OF NOT KNOWING

Linger in the space of
not knowing—
stay longer, stay with
me
in the space of
wisdom.

If you dream of
reason,
you are dreaming.

NO GOOD

Well what do I do with you
        if there is no single good
What do you do with me
        if there is no single good
What do we do with the world
        if there is no single good
What can we do for each other
        if there is no single good
How do we decide
        if there is no single good
Aren't we destined to fail
        if there is no single good
Will our ego take a hit
        if there is no single good
Won't our ego fall
        if there is no single good
Is it the only good
        that there is no single good?

DOGMA

Life steers us
making sure
we grow hesitant
about things
once beyond
question.

LAUGH

"I can't imagine myself anywhere else"
is an invitation for the gods
to ruffle our feathers—
so that we start imagining.

THOUGHTS

Stop worshipping false idols, false thoughts.
Thoughts are created to be
false creatures.

BELIEF

Whatever
you believe
is what will
get you
in trouble.

The greatest
deception
we have
is an
opinion

and yet
the world
maintains its
own intricate
balance through
your own telling
of the truth.

TRUTH

We tell the truth, our stories.
And yet the truth
lies beyond—
in the space between bodies,
between private infinities
we call bodies.

FOUNDATION

How unbearable
to live in a universe
in which pain
is a source of
growth.

Other options
please?

COMPASSION

I'm sorry only for my
thoughts—
sorry for the years of
disdain toward all
the beings
I would later
become.

KRISHNA

There is a story of Baby Krishna playing in the mud. He takes some of the mud and puts it in his mouth. His mother reprimands, "Stop that. Spit that out." Baby Krishna opens his mouth and there she sees earth, but also the whole earth—in all of its entirety. She sees birth and destruction. She sees love and hate. The violence, the eternity, the cosmos, the spaciousness. She is overwhelmed and physically closes the baby's mouth.

Maybe the secrets that I
kept like extra buttons
were just another
face of God.

OCEAN

Something is always fading in and fading out.
Love is always beginning or ending.
Waves recede, waves advance,
waves evaporate, waves rain down.
The ocean freezes, cracks, melts,
inundates, and freezes again.
Our souls go from liquid to solid to air.

FIELD OF POSSIBILITY

Suddenly hanging in the
air like fame.
Count yourself in,
rejoicing, and then
demolish the count.

Every hour that goes by is
younger

in every moment
you are still
unknown.

CHRISTIANITY

If you turn the other cheek
are you not just
propagating evil?

REFLECTION

It's not punitive
by a God in the clouds,
it's reflective.

Reality is a mirror
thanks to the
law of karma.

Love thy neighbor
as thyself.

(Not judge
not force
not flagellate
not criticize
not control
not condemn
without a trial

Love.)
A clean mirror
reflects back love.

TIME

In space lies the infinite

The infinite lies in space
it is there
one inside the other

    both present always

    the infinite and space inside the infinite
    space and the infinite inside space

Only time doesn't exist

because if there's space and the infinite—
                                        how can it?

HAPPINESS

Happiness is
praying
thank you
more often
than
praying
please

without
giving it
a thought

SIDDHARTHA

Hope you have many names
so they encompass
all that you are.

Serenity and chaos.

The sound of water
says what I think.

Serenity and chaos.

Hope you have as many names
as sounds of water flowing.

Serenity and chaos.

Sound of water
closer to light than logic.

Serenity and chaos.

SUFFERING

Suffering will not pass us by
there's not a lot we know
but we know
that suffering will not pass us by
it will keep going
new suffering will find us,
old suffering will let go
(sometimes, sometimes not)
and new joy will find us
and old suffering will release
and new suffering will find us
and new joy will find us
and old suffering will release

ONESELF

people betray themselves
to try to be
happy

after people
betray
themselves

they are very rarely
happy

NON-DUALITY

ugliness moves to beauty
and back.

what is useless can move to
what is profoundly useful
and even redeeming
and back.

entropy
nothingness
atrophy

rich
viscous
potent

and back.

INFINITE

Because one is finite
a departure from this place always feels final;
leaving it behind is leaving it forever.

Because one is infinite
a departure from this place is never final;
we only leave it for a moment
there are always second chances.

BUDDHA

You can't get there
with any light
other than
your own.

AFTERWORD

"Divinity School" is a great title for a book of poems: at first glance, it appears familiar—even comforting. Yet almost immediately, that initial reassurance becomes the site of growing tension. The title seems to promise a structure of ancient, solid, well-established knowledge, only to subject the reader (the student?) to forty-four disquieting texts. In poems such as "Eve," paradise is exposed as fiction; in "Gabriel," the angels of the Annunciation are likened to "vultures." In this respect, the subtitle feels almost misplaced: it seems to sidestep the profound disruption the book ultimately enacts.

The title is certainly true to the book in that it signals its meticulous unity and coherence: no *doubt* that all poems in this book engage with the divine and its schooling, while at the same time "doubt," uneasiness, uncertainty, hesitation, and most words in that family, contribute in equal measure to the unity of the book with their sustained unsettling of all things divine. As does "truth" or, rather, the relentless interrogation of truth in ever-widening circles.

From a more formal or structural perspective, additional elements reinforce the book's unity. For example, the poems are marked by brevity and precision, and especially by a distinctive mode of closure. Their endings often introduce an unexpected turn—sometimes subtle, sometimes abrupt. A poem may conclude with a humorous or colloquial phrase that overturns the gravity of its subject, as in "Joseph," with its wry and decidedly secular rejection of the conventional Nativity scene. Elsewhere, the ending may open the tradition under scrutiny to new "possibilities" (a concept intriguingly explored in some poems); it is the case of the last line in "Foundation": "Other options / please?" Or it may dismantle the poem's governing premise altogether, as in "Christ," who would need to relinquish the title of savior in order to preserve his freedom.

But this elegant, unconventional *Divinity School* does more than revisit a set of doctrines. It does not merely pose a new understanding of faith or faithlessness nor simply bend inherited wisdom. Ultimately, this collection of poems sketches, in an almost biographical manner, a series of steps in a life of meaning, thus inviting the reader to ponder precisely that: the continual probing that lies at the heart of any deeply spiritual life.

Luis Fernández Cifuentes
Cambridge MA, March 2026

Professor of Romance Languages & Literatures Harvard University, Faculty of Arts and Sciences

Former Chair of the Romance Languages & Literatures Department

YOUR JOURNEY: NEXT STEPS

The goal of poetry is to bring us closer to ourselves and the divine. It is a source of human happiness.

If you want to take the next steps on your journey to happiness with Elizabeth through meditation, ancient wisdom, and science of the mind, you are welcome to participate in the Journey.

You are also invited to receive
daily inspiring texts from Elizabeth.

More information at **www.happinessangha.com**.

www.ingramcontent.com/pod-product-compliance
Lightning Source LLC
LaVergne TN
LVHW042357150826
845671LV00023B/381/J